moment
meditations

WHISPERS of PRAYER

Emilie Barnes

Harvest House Publishers
Eugene, Oregon

Whispers of Prayer
Copyright © 1999 Harvest House Publishers
Eugene, Oregon 97402

ISBN 0-7369-0031-4

Text is adapted from 15 *Minutes Alone with God* by
Emilie Barnes (Harvest House Publishers, 1994).

Design and production by Left Coast Design, Portland, Oregon.
Artwork by Gwen Babbitt

Unless otherwise indicated, Scripture quotations are from the
Holy Bible, New International Version ®, Copyright © 1973,
1978, 1984 by the International Bible Society. Used by permis-
sion of Zondervan Publishing House. Scripture quotations
marked KJV are from the King James Version of the Bible.

Printed in China.

99 00 01 02 03 04 05 06 07 08 / PP / 10 9 8 7 6 5 4 3 2 1

*T*o every woman who wants to get in touch with her Lord and life, may this book be an encouragement to you. Take a few minutes to close the door on another busy day as you make time for the Lord and listen to His call. He will lead you to a special quiet time of spiritual refreshment and endless peace, to the source of constant comfort and unending love, to Himself.

To our darling daughter — thought there are some neat 'take-a-deep-breath' "whispers" here — with love always Mom

8/31/01

I will call on him
as long as I live.
PSALM 116:2

*Y*ou don't have to make an appointment to ask God for something you need or to thank Him for something you have received. He is interested in everything that happens to you.

• • ● • •

Prayer is talking with God and telling Him you love Him, conversing with God about all the things that are important in life, both large and small, and being assured that He is listening.

C. NEIL STRAIT

When you pray, go into your room, close the door and pray to your Father, who is unseen.

MATTHEW 6:6

• • • • •

Father God, may I never forget to call on You in every situation. I want to call on You every day of my life. Thank You for being within the sound of my voice and only a thought's distance away. Amen.

• • • • •

When your day is hemmed with prayer it is less likely to unravel.

SOURCE UNKNOWN

Gwendolyn Babbitt © 1991

The fruit of the Spirit is. . . .

GALATIANS 5:22

· · • · ·

Which of us doesn't need a touch of God's love, patience, kindness, goodness, gentleness, and self-control in our lives? Those are the things as well as guidance, wisdom, hope, and a deeper knowledge of Him that He wants to give us as His children.

Love is the greatest thing that God can give us; for he is love: and it is the greatest thing we can give to God.

JEREMY TAYLOR

Father God, thank You for all You do for my family. May they continue to love You, serve You, honor and devour Your Word. I pray that they will be filled with knowledge, spiritual understanding, and wisdom. May they walk in Your steps. Amen.

· · ● · ·

Make two homes for thyself...
One actual home...
and another spiritual home,
which thou art to
carry with thee always.

LETTER TO ST. CATHERINE OF SIENA

*By wisdom a house
is built, and through
understanding it
is established.*
PROVERBS 24:3

Be joyful always;
pray continually;
give thanks in all
circumstances, for
this is God's
will for you in
Christ Jesus.

1 THESSALONIANS
5:16-18

Make it your priority to spend time with God daily. There's not a single right time or correct place. The only requirement is your willing heart.

. . ● . .

Lord! Thou knowest how busy I must be this day: if I forget thee, do not thou forget me.

SIR JACOB ASTLEY

*F*ather God, thank you for reminding me that it's the little things that count in life. Let me dwell on this truth today. I sometimes get so caught up in the big things that I forget the preciousness of simplicity. Amen.

A soul that is capable of knowing God can be filled with nothing else but God.

JEREMIAH BURROWS

Blessed are the pure in heart, for they will see God.
MATTHEW 5:8

*Casting all your
care upon him, for
he careth for you.*
1 PETER 5:7 KJV

God has made it clear that He is interested in us who are His children. Talk to Him as you would to your earthly parent or a special friend who loves you, desires the best for you, and wants to help you in every way possible.

• • • • •

Do not make prayer a monologue—make it a conversation.

SOURCE UNKNOWN

Prayer casts light and hope
into the dark corners of your life.

• • ● • •

It is from prayer that the Spirit's victory springs.

SCHILLERBUCH

*Thy word is a lamp
unto my feet, and a light
unto my path.*

PSALM 119:105 KJV

Be imitators of
God, therefore,
as dearly loved
children.
EPHESIANS 5:1

*F*ather God, oh You know how I want to be like You. The deepest part of my heart and soul aches for Your wisdom. May today be a special day for new revelation. Amen.

• • • • •

Take God for your spouse
and friend and walk with
Him continually, and
you will not sin and
will learn to love, and
the things you must
do will work out
prosperously for you.

SAINT JOHN
OF THE CROSS

When we find ourselves looking to the future because we aren't content with today, may God give us a peace of mind that lets us rest where He has placed us.

. . . . .

My God, give me neither poverty nor riches, but whatsoever it may be Thy will to give, give me with it a heart that knows humbly to acquiesce in what is Thy will.

FRANCOIS DE LA
ROCHEFOUCAULD

But godliness with contentment is great gain.
1 TIMOTHY 6:6

A friend loves

at all times.

PROVERBS

17:17

*F*ather God, thank You for friends who stand beside me in all situations. They are always there when I need them to listen, laugh, and cry. They are so special to my life. May they realize what their friendship means to me. Amen.

• • • • •

Nothing purchased can come close to the renewed sense of gratitude for having family and friends.

COURTLAND MILLOY

*H*ow many of us have a poem to be written, a song to be sung, a book to be authored? Listen to God today as He calls you to a life of adventure.

• • ● • •

A man should be encouraged to do what the Maker of him has intended by the making of him, according as the gifts have been bestowed on him for that purpose.

THOMAS CARLYLE

Well done, good and

faithful servant!

MATTHEW 25:21

Always giving thanks to God the Father for everything.

EPHESIANS 5:20

In the morning upon waking, thank God for another day, good health, and purpose for life. In the evening upon retiring, thank God for watching over you, giving you a meaningful day, and providing safety, food, and shelter.

• • ● • •

Do not have your concert first and tune your instruments afterward. Begin the day with God.

JAMES HUDSON TAYLOR

*F*ather God, put a strong desire in my soul to spend time with You today in prayer and study. Let time stand still and let me forget all about my watch and schedule. Amen.

• • ● • •

Where there is peace and meditation,
there is neither anxiety nor doubt.

SAINT FRANCIS OF ASSISI

Whom have I in heaven but you? And being with you, I desire nothing on earth.

PSALM 73:25

How much more will your Father in

heaven give good gifts to those who ask him!

MATTHEW 7:11

We certainly have the opportunity to experience the abundance of God if we are willing to ask. Your Father in heaven is waiting to give you good gifts if you will ask Him.

• • • • •

God's gifts put man's best dreams to shame.

ELIZABETH BARRETT BROWNING

Life is like a race. We must discipline ourselves to study and know God's Word, but exciting results come later when our hearts begin to produce a harvest of righteousness and peace. We become mature, strong, and able to help others.

• • • • •

The study of God's Word, for the purpose of discovering God's will, is the secret discipline which has formed the greatest characters.

JAMES W. ALEXANDER

Let us run with

perseverance the race

marked out for us.

HEBREWS 12:1

We will tell the next generation

the praiseworthy deeds of the Lord.

PSALM 78:4

Lord God, I thank You for the godly men and women You have put in my life. They have been an inspiration to my Christian growth. Help me to continually seek out those godly people who will live the Christian walk in front of me. Amen.

* * * * *

Seek the Lord. Keep seeking through prayer, Bible study, and fellowship with other Christians. Give Him an opportunity to multiply what He gave you.

CORRIE TEN BOOM

*W*hen we come before God with an open heart and a voice of confession, He is just and will forgive us. With this emptying of our old self, He will give us a new song. He will give you a new song, one written just for you.

• • • • •

God can do wonders with a broken heart
if you give him all the pieces.

VICTOR ALFSEN

He put a new song in my mouth, a hymn of praise to our God.

PSALM 40:3

"For I know the plans I have for you," declares the Lord.

JEREMIAH 29:11

*F*ather God, create in me a hunger to search out Your plan for my life. Let me have the wisdom to major on the majors and not get sidetracked by the minors. When life is over I want You to say, "Well done, good and faithful servant." Amen.

• • ● • •

We must not make our own plans without God's guidance. Do your planning while in prayer.

CORRIE TEN BOOM

I am not ashamed of the gospel, because it is the power of God for the salvation of everyone who believes.

ROMANS 1:16

The gospel is a change agent, helping us against the power of sin, giving people real purpose and meaning to life.

• • • • •

That God is more near, more real and more mighty, more full of love, and more ready to help every one of us than anyone of us realizes, is the undying message.

DAVID S. CAIRNS

The heavens declare the

glory of God: the skies

proclaim the work

of his hands.

PSALM 19:1

*F*ather God, thank You for the simple reminders of who You are and what You have done. You are a great and awesome God. Help me to remember that always. Amen.

• • ● • •

The resolved mind hath no cares.

GEORGE HERBERT

We're not finished yet—far from it. Growing in godliness is a lifelong process.

• • • • •

Our lives will be complete only when we express the full intent of the Master.

CHARLES R. HEMBREE

Therefore, if anyone is in Christ, he is a new

creation; the old has gone, the new has come!

2 CORINTHIANS 5:17

Even when I am
old and gray, do
not forsake me,
O God, till
I declare your
power to the
next generation.
PSALM 71:18

ord, continue to give us a message, give us a passion for the message, power to tell the message, and an audience to hear it.

· · ● · ·

I believe that the desire to please You does in fact please You. And I hope I have that desire in all I am doing.

THOMAS MERTON

Be still, and know that I am God.

PSALM 46:10

We must seek out opportunities to rest, plan, regroup, and draw closer to God.

Deliberately cultivate the spirit of stillness in your home and in your life.

• • • • •

How can you expect God to speak in that gentle and inward voice which melts the soul, when you are making so much noise with your rapid reflections? Be silent, and God will speak again.

FRANCOIS DE LA
MOTHE FÉNELON

Gwendolyn Babbitt © 1991

Noah found favor in the eyes of the Lord.

GENESIS 6:8

*F*ather God, oh may I find favor with You. Give me a hunger to fall in love with Your Word and put it to work in my life. Amen.

• • ● • •

Jesus Christ opens wide the doors of the treasure-house of God's promises, and bids us go in and take with boldness the riches that are ours.

CORRIE TEN BOOM

*H*ospitality goes beyond friends and neighbors. Invite a visiting missionary or evangelist home for a meal. Host members of a visiting choir or a work team that's away from home. Whatever the need, reach out and extend your hand of hospitality.

• • ● • •

*Obedience to our
Heavenly Father starts
with our loving service
to a needy brother.*

WILLIAM WARD

Offer hospitality to one another.
1 Peter 4:9

I praise you because I am fearfully and wonderfully made.
PSALM 139:14

$\mathcal{F}$ather God, help me to realize that I am truly and marvelously made and that, in Your sight, I am very special. Amen.

• • ● • •

Fearfullty and wonderfully He made this new creation which He had planned from the beginning of time ...He breathed into this earthen pot the breath of life and it became a living being.

NEIL T. ANDERSON

*I*f you spend time alone with God in the morning, you'll start your day refreshed and ready for whatever comes your way. If you spend time alone with Him in the evening, you'll go to sleep relaxed, resting in His care and ready for a new day to serve Him.

. . • . .

Prayer is not a substitute for work, thinking, watching, suffering, or giving; prayer is a support for all other efforts.

GEORGE BUTTRICK

Jesus . . .

went off to a

solitary place,

where he

prayed.

MARK 1:35

You will seek me and find me when

you seek me with all your heart.

JEREMIAH 29:13

*F*ather God, I want to be a woman
who seeks after Your knowledge.
Show me Your ways that I might
acknowledge You as God. Help me to see
that You are all that I will ever need.
Amen.

• • • • •

*God always answers us in
the deeps, never in the
shallows of our soul.*

<small>AMY CARMICHAEL</small>

Come to God's altar and lay the pain of your heart there. Stop and worship. And as you walk away, you will know with hope and trust that God says, "I will provide."

• • • • •

I know Christ dwells within me all the time, guiding me and inspiring me whenever I do or say anything. A light of which I caught no glimmer before comes to me at the very moment when it is needed.

SAINT THERESE OF LISIEUX

And Abraham called the name of that place Jehovah-jireh: as it is said to this day, In the mount of the Lord it shall be seen.

GENESIS 22:14 KJV

Charm is deceptive, and beauty

is fleeting; but a woman who fears

the Lord is to be praised.

PROVERBS 31:30

• • ● • •

ather God, You know that my heart's desire is to be a godly woman. Show me Your way today. Let me be a beautiful fragrance that blesses the lives of others. Amen.

• • ● • •

The only thing you will take through those pearly gates is what you have given away.

MARCIA MOORE